CW01512944

Original title:
Mossy Rays Inside the Faerie Ledge

Author: Eliora Lumiste
ISBN HARDBACK: 978-1-80562-423-3
ISBN PAPERBACK: 978-1-80563-944-2

Whispers of Green Beneath Celestial Beams

In the hush of dawn's embrace,
Leaves whisper secrets of the place.
Sunlight dances on the stream,
As shadows weave a waking dream.

Gentle breezes carry lore,
Of ancient woods and evermore.
Ferns unfurl to greet the light,
In a world where magic takes flight.

Mushrooms peek from earthy beds,
While butterflies lift their tender red.
Each rustle tells a tale untold,
Of nights in silver and days of gold.

Enchanted Glimmers in the Woodland Shade

Underneath the verdant boughs,
Where silence wears a soothing blouse.
Glimmers dance on mossy stone,
In the heart of woods, we're not alone.

The air hangs thick with secrets veiled,
In softly woven paths we sailed.
Twinkling lights like fireflies play,
Guiding wanderers on their way.

Faint laughter ripples through the trees,
Carried on a warming breeze.
If you listen, you may find,
The enchantment of the forest kind.

Secrets of the Sylvan Glade

Where shadows stretch in dappled light,
The sylvan glade holds dreams in sight.
Every rustle speaks of fate,
Soft echoes that the woods create.

Cloaked in whispers and in shade,
The spirit of the forest stayed.
Willows sway with tales to tell,
Their branches weave a magic spell.

Night unfolds with starry sighs,
While the moonbeams softly rise.
In this tranquil, hallowed ground,
The mysteries of life are found.

The Glint of Leaves in Twilight's Embrace

As daylight wanes and shadows creep,
The leaves glint bright, their secrets deep.
In twilight's soft and silver glow,
Nature's wonders start to flow.

With every sigh, the night awakes,
As gentle whispers weave like flakes.
The forest stirs, its breath is light,
Guiding spirits through the night.

Stars peek through the canopy,
Embroidered in a tapestry.
With every flicker, they will show,
The magic realms that ebb and flow.

Hidden Illumination in the Thicket

In shadows deep where secrets lie,
Soft whispers weave 'neath the twilight sky.
The thicket holds a magic rare,
With hidden lights that dance in air.

Old trees stand tall, their branches sway,
Guardians of night, keeping watch till day.
Yet in the dark, a flicker glows,
As nature's heart in silence knows.

A river babbles, bright and clear,
It sings of dreams that linger near.
With every pulse, the night takes flight,
Illumination breaks the night.

Dew-kissed leaves with gems adorned,
Each droplet tells of night reborn.
The thicket's song, in hushed delight,
Holds hidden truths wrapped in light.

So wander softly, tread with care,
For magic dwells in stillness there.
In every rustle, a tale begins,
Of joy and warmth within the sins.

A Symphony of Nature's Glimmers

Beneath the stars, a harmony blooms,
In fragrant fields where night perfume looms.
Crickets play on a silver string,
A symphony made for the wandering.

Moonlight spills on dance of leaf,
Each flicker whispers tales of belief.
In every rustle, a voice does stir,
Songs of darkness that shift and blur.

With every note, the night unfolds,
Stories of wonders long retold.
The wind joins in, a gentle choir,
Breathing hope, igniting fire.

Amidst the thrills of gentle sighs,
Glimmers of truth weave in the skies.
Each shimmer, like a heart set free,
In rhythmic pulse, a symphony.

So close your eyes, and let it flow,
This chant of life, soft and slow.
For in the night, the world resounds,
A tapestry where joy abounds.

Faerie Lights Amidst the Quiet Grove

In twilight hours, the faeries bloom,
With laughter bright, dispelling gloom.
They dance beneath the ancient trees,
Whispering secrets to evening's breeze.

A gentle glow, they weave in flight,
Painting shadows with strokes of light.
In hidden nooks, enchantments play,
As dusk embraces the end of day.

Softly they flit on wings of grace,
In every heart, they find a place.
The grove alive with faerie cheer,
Elysium, where dreams appear.

Each flicker shows a path to roam,
Illuminating the lost, the lone.
In their realm, all fears take flight,
As faerie lights guide through the night.

So linger long, let spirits soar,
In the quiet grove, you'll find much more.
With every twinkle, love does thrive,
In faerie lights, the world's alive.

The Brush of Gold on Green

Morning breaks with a golden hue,
The brush of light on emerald dew.
Nature awakens from dreams so deep,
As sunlight stirs the world from sleep.

Beneath the trees with trunks so stout,
Lies a carpet where shadows flout.
Each blade of grass, a glistening gem,
In this tapestry, life roots and stems.

With gentle touch, the sun bestows,
A thousand secrets, the heart knows.
In whispers soft, the lilies sway,
Grateful for the warmth of day.

The breeze carries the scent of bloom,
In every garden, dispelling gloom.
A brush of gold meets green divine,
A painter's dream, a grand design.

So linger here, amongst the trees,
Let the sunlight dance with ease.
For in this moment, pure and clear,
The brush of gold brings joy, sincere.

Kaleidoscope of Bark and Bark

In the forest where shadows dance,
Mossy carpets weave their trance.
Branches twist in playful guise,
Drawing secrets 'neath the skies.

Colors shift with each fresh breeze,
Nature whispers through the trees.
Rings of history etched so deep,
Guarding dreams the ancients keep.

Textures tell a tale untold,
Of creatures fierce and moments bold.
Knots and grooves entwined with fate,
In this grove, magic isn't late.

Underneath the velvet night,
Stars will twinkle with delight.
Every whisper, every spark,
Hides a story in the bark.

Spirits of the Glade's Glow

In the heart of the green glade,
Moonlight paints a silver shade.
Whispers echo soft and low,
Spirits dance in gentle flow.

Flickering lights like fireflies,
Guide the way beneath the skies.
Moss-lined paths where shadows weave,
Invite the dreamers to believe.

Elfin laughter fills the air,
Magic twirls with midnight flair.
Nature's symphony, sweet and clear,
Calls to hearts to draw them near.

Golden ferns and silver streams,
Cradle softly all our dreams.
In this haven, souls unite,
Finding peace in lavish night.

A Tapestry of Light and Leaves

Threads of green and gold entwined,
Nature's canvas, bright and kind.
Whispers of the wind unite,
Weaving day into the night.

Sunbeams filter through the trees,
Painting shadows with the breeze.
Memory in every vein,
Tales of sunshine and of rain.

Petals fall like notes of song,
Returning to where they belong.
Each leaf tells of seasons passed,
Of moments fleeting, ever vast.

In this tapestry so grand,
Life's intricate and steady hand.
Every hue a story spun,
Underneath the warming sun.

Serenade of the Woodland Spirits

Amid the oaks, a melody,
Sings of love and mystery.
Gentle notes on evening air,
Cushioned by the softest care.

Stars above begin to gleam,
Whispering beneath the dream.
In the hush, the spirits sway,
Guiding night to greet the day.

Faintest echoes twist and twirl,
Dancing leaves in happy whirl.
Nature hums a soothing tune,
Beneath the watchful gaze of moon.

Lost in time, the woodlands breathe,
Offering warmth, a sweet reprieve.
Every shadow, every light,
Murmurs secrets of the night.

Celestial Hues in the Leave's Embrace

In a forest where the shadows play,
Leaves shimmer with a golden ray.
Bright emerald and russet collide,
Nature's canvas, a vivid guide.

The breeze murmurs secrets untold,
Carrying dreams both young and old.
Each gust a whisper of ancient lore,
Inviting hearts to explore.

Sunlight filters through branches wide,
Creating paths where magic hides.
A tapestry woven with care,
In this realm, enchantment's rare.

Flickering lights dance on the ground,
In nature's symphony, joy is found.
Moments captured in every hue,
A world alive, forever new.

As day folds into twilight's embrace,
Stars awaken, filling the space.
Celestial glow in the leaves' fold,
An eternal story yet untold.

Gentle Luminance on Nature's Carpet

Morning dew on the emerald blades,
Glitters softly as daylight fades.
Flecks of light in a tender dance,
Each droplet cast in a dreamy trance.

Dappled sunlight spills through the trees,
Whispers carried upon the breeze.
Nature's breath sings a soft refrain,
A melody sweet, as pure as rain.

Cascading colors, a painter's delight,
Brooks babble sweetly, hearts taking flight.
Every petal a promise of spring,
In this retreat, the soul takes wing.

Shadows entwine amidst the bloom,
Elixirs of joy dissolve all gloom.
With every step, a story to find,
The touch of magic, gentle and kind.

As sun bows low in the velvet sky,
Hues transform, a colorful sigh.
A tapestry woven with tenderness,
Nature whispers its sweet caress.

Hidden Haven of Whispered Gleams

Nestled deep where the wild things dwell,
A hidden haven casts its spell.
Silent echoes of laughter ring,
In the arms of twilight, fairies sing.

A brook giggles over smooth stones,
Each drop a secret, the forest's tones.
Beneath the boughs, shadows blend,
In this refuge where magic transcends.

Moonlight spills on the forest floor,
A shimmering path to explore.
Starlit whispers twinkling bright,
Guiding the lost through the night.

Night's embrace wraps all so tight,
Guarding dreams until first light.
In this haven, all fears cease,
A sanctuary steeped in peace.

Time stands still within this glade,
Infectious laughter will never fade.
Forever this magic shall gleam,
A refuge shaped of every dream.

Embrace of the Sunlit Hollow

In a hollow where the sunlight spills,
Golden warmth on the rolling hills.
Nature's breath lingers soft and bright,
In the embrace of the morning light.

Petals unfurl in colors rare,
Inviting hearts to breathe the air.
Every blossom whispers a tale,
Of timeless love that will not fail.

The brook runs swiftly, a silver thread,
Winding whispers where the wanderers tread.
All paths converge, hearts intertwine,
In this tranquil space, all is divine.

Breezes tease with a playful song,
Drawing wanderers to linger long.
Soft laughter echoes through the trees,
A serenade kissed by the breeze.

As shadows lengthen, colors fade,
The sun dips low, a grand parade.
This sunlit hollow, forever bright,
A cherished home in the arms of light.

Fables Unfold in Emerald Nooks

In the heart of emerald woods,
Whispers weave through ancient trees.
Stories linger in the shadows,
Like secrets carried on the breeze.

Mysteries wrapped in green embrace,
A dance of light through leafy bower.
Tales of kin and age-old friends,
Awaken here, in twilight's hour.

A fox with eyes like amber stars,
Guides the wanderers with gentle grace.
Through thickets thick and hollows deep,
He reveals a hidden place.

Mossy stones hum songs of old,
As sunlight filters soft and low.
Each step, a tune, each breath, a tale,
In the glades where fables grow.

Beneath the boughs, the stories twine,
In emerald nooks their magic lies.
Gather ye close and lend an ear,
To the soft sigh of twilight skies.

Dappled Light Upon Velvet Earth

Dappled light on velvet earth,
Kisses the ground where dreams are spun.
A tapestry of shadowed hues,
Beneath the warmth of setting sun.

Petals drift like whispered words,
Carried by a gentle sigh.
In the hush, a promise glows,
As night unfurls its velvet sky.

A brook reflects a silver gleam,
Its laughter dances with the trees.
Each ripple holds a story told,
In the rustling of the leaves.

In the corners where the wild things play,
Magic stirs in fragrant air.
Silent wonders greet the dusk,
In the twilight, feelings rare.

Kissed by starlight, dreams take flight,
In the realm where secrets merge.
Dappled light upon velvet earth,
In hearts, the echoes surge.

Echoes of Magic in Nature's Cradle

In cradle soft of nature's arms,
Whispers curl like smoke in air.
Echoes of magic dance with wind,
In the stillness, spirits share.

The forest hums a lullaby,
With notes of joy and tales of woe.
Every stone, a keeper wise,
Of memories from long ago.

Where wildflowers paint the ground,
With colors bright and scents dewy,
Each petal's brush is pure delight,
In nature's heart, a shimmering hue.

Beneath the branches, shadows play,
With echoes of laughter, soft and warm.
Magic swirls in quiet corners,
In every breeze, a latent charm.

Let your spirit wander free,
In the cradle of the green and gold.
For echoes of magic dwell within,
A universe of stories told.

The Hidden Glow of Dreaming Ferns

In twilight's hush, where ferns hold dreams,
A secret glow begins to rise.
Soft green fronds with stories breathe,
Beneath the cloak of starry skies.

They whisper tales of gentle rains,
When moonbeams dance on dew-kissed leaves.
Each frond, a bridge to worlds unknown,
Where every heart seeks what it believes.

In the quiet of the emerald glade,
Fables weave in the night's embrace.
With every flicker, shadows play,
Their stories etched in nature's grace.

The hidden glow of dreaming ferns,
Lights the path for those who roam.
In the stillness, magic stirs,
Reminding us we are not alone.

So tread with care, dear-hearted soul,
And listen close to the story's end.
For in the fern's soft, glowing hold,
Lies the warmth of a faithful friend.

Luminous Secrets Beneath The Boughs

Beneath the boughs of emerald green,
Whispers of magic remain unseen.
Each rustling leaf tells tales of old,
Of dreams unspoken, and secrets bold.

Light dances softly on the forest floor,
Inviting the curious to explore.
With every step, the shadows play,
And hidden wonders beckon to stay.

A glint of gold in a sunbeam's kiss,
A fleeting moment of purest bliss.
The heart of the wood beats strong and true,
Bound by the stories of ages anew.

In the stillness, a soft sigh breaks,
The ancient trees stir, their slumber shakes.
As dusk begins to weave its thread,
Luminous secrets fill hearts with dread.

Here, the enchantment lingers long,
In the symphony of the wild birds' song.
For those who seek with open hearts,
The luminous secrets that nature imparts.

Serenity in the Shade of Ancient Trees

In the embrace of giants, shadows lie,
Where whispers of wind and dreams comply.
Leaves like lace sway gently in tune,
Cradling the light of the silver moon.

A tranquil hush blankets the grove,
Nature's own promise of peace, a trove.
Golden dappled sun in a lazy dance,
Invites the weary for a sunlit trance.

Every gnarled branch holds history's weight,
Silent witness to the hands of fate.
Beneath their canopies, hearts unwind,
Serenity found, leaving woes behind.

Soft moss cushions weary feet,
In this sanctuary, time feels discreet.
The scent of pine drifts sweet on the breeze,
Wrapping around hopes, granting gentle ease.

In the shade where the old trees stand tall,
Each sigh of the forest weaves a call.
For those who pause, their spirits rise,
Serenity blooms under quiet skies.

Traces of Enchantment Amidst the Ferns

Amidst the ferns, a softness glows,
Where echoes of laughter the woodland knows.
A carpet of green sways in delight,
Holding the magic of day and night.

In every curl, a tale unfolds,
Of pixie dances and heroes bold.
The dew-kissed leaves carry secrets rare,
Whispers of dreams linger in the air.

Footfalls whisper on the mossy ground,
In this hidden realm, enchantment's found.
With every breath, a spell is spun,
As sunlight filters, and shadows run.

The ancient trees, their silhouettes lean,
Guardians of wonders, both felt and seen.
A flicker of light, a shimmering haze,
Traces of magic in intricate ways.

So wander forth where the ferns grow deep,
Into the silence where dreams may creep.
For those who seek with open hearts,
Traces of enchantment dwell in the arts.

Celestial Beams Through the Canopy's Veil

Through the canopy's veil, the light breaks free,
Casting celestial beams, wild and free.
A dance of shadows on the forest's skin,
The sacred stillness welcomes you in.

Each ray, a whisper from the stars above,
Guiding lost souls with a gentle love.
In this hallowed space, your spirit soars,
Awash in the glow of the forest's cores.

The branches sway with a timeless grace,
In this enchanted, ethereal place.
Beneath the glowing arch, hearts entwine,
Touched by the silk of the divine.

As dusk falls softly, the colors blend,
Day's gentle farewell, as night descends.
In the quiet, the whispers of dreams ignite,
The celestial beams meet the approaching night.

So linger awhile where the world feels whole,
Let the forest's magic unfurl your soul.
For in every beam, a story is sewn,
Celestial whispers, in the silence, grown.

Faerie Dreams in a Sunlit Hollow

In a glade where shadows play,
Whispers of the fae do sway,
Glimmers twirl in morning mist,
Nature's warmth, a gentle tryst.

Amber light through leaves does dance,
Spirits twirl in playful chance,
Every petal, every dew,
Sings of dreams both bright and true.

Flowers bloom with colors bright,
Echoes of a secret night,
In their hearts, a magic stirs,
Softly sung by silver furs.

Breezes weave a tender song,
Where the faerie folk belong,
Cocooned in the morning's grace,
Lost in dreams, a fleeting space.

As the sun begins to fade,
In the hollow, magic's made,
Stars will weave a tapestry,
Of faerie dreams, wild and free.

The Dance of Light and Moss

In the forest, green and deep,
Where the ancient secrets keep,
Sunlight dapples on the ground,
Whispers float without a sound.

Mossy carpets soft and cool,
Nature's lush, enchanting jewel,
Here the dance of light does play,
Guiding hearts that lost their way.

Ferns unfurl with gentle grace,
In this serene, enchanted space,
Every step a soft embrace,
In the woods, the shadows trace.

Light and moss begin to twine,
In this realm, the worlds align,
Every flicker, every glow,
Sings of magic, soft and slow.

As twilight wraps its silky shroud,
In the hush, I stand and bow,
Grateful for the wondrous sight,
Of the dance of moss and light.

Ethereal Darkness Graced by Light

In a world where shadows linger,
Darkness holds a silver finger,
Stars will wink from velvet skies,
Illuminating whispered sighs.

Haunting echoes softly drift,
Through the night, a precious gift,
Shimmers of a fleeting glow,
In the dark, the heart will know.

Light does filter through the trees,
Weaving tales upon the breeze,
Every night, a canvas cast,
Where the present meets the past.

Here the mysteries unfold,
In the silence, stories told,
Finding beauty, pure and bright,
In the depths of endless night.

As dreams take flight on whispered wings,
Ethereal, the nightingale sings,
Guiding souls through shadow's grace,
Finding light in dark's embrace.

Nature's Canvas of Brief Radiance

Upon the hill, where wild things bloom,
Nature paints with colors' plume,
Every stroke, a fleeting gift,
As time's currents gently drift.

Petals sigh in vibrant hues,
Kissed by sunlight's golden dues,
In the breeze, a moment's song,
Nature's heart beats wild and strong.

Clouds drift past in soft delight,
Casting shadows, framing light,
Every dawn, a brand-new chance,
To witness life's enchanting dance.

Through each season's swirling breath,
Beauty blooms, defying death,
A canvas made of love and care,
Where magic lingers in the air.

As twilight paints the sky with fire,
On this canvas, hearts aspire,
To capture moments, rich and rare,
In nature's breath, we find our prayer.

Faerie Whims Among the Ferns

In the hush where shadows play,
Tiny whispers dance and sway,
Glimmers bright on dew-kissed spheres,
The faeries laugh beyond our years.

A hidden path of emerald lays,
Softly woven, secret ways,
With each step, a spell is spun,
In this realm, all hearts are won.

Stars beneath the leafy dome,
Where fabled creatures find their home,
Wings of silver, flashes bright,
In the soft embrace of night.

Time stands still, in softest hues,
With every breath, a world renews,
Ferns and flowers gently sway,
In harmony with night and day.

Here beneath the ancient trees,
Hopes are carried on the breeze,
Heartfelt wishes take their flight,
In the hush of faerie light.

The Glade's Tender Embrace

Amidst the trees, in silence found,
A sacred glade, where dreams abound,
Soft moss carpets the shaded floor,
In nature's cradle, spirits soar.

Sunlight dances through the leaves,
Weaving tapestries that it weaves,
Whispers of lore in gentle streams,
Waking the echoes of our dreams.

Flowers bloom in vibrant hues,
Painting stories in morning dew,
The symphony of the wild calls,
As twilight drapes its velvet shawls.

Here, the brook sings sweet and clear,
Every note a song to hear,
Nature's lullaby softly flows,
Binding hearts as twilight glows.

In this realm, all worries cease,
A moment's pause, a tender peace,
The glade's embrace, a gift so dear,
Where every soul finds solace here.

Fragments of Light in Murky Depths

Beneath the ripples, shadows weave,
A hidden world, where few believe,
Glimmers flicker in darkened waves,
A place where light and magic saves.

Mysteries lurk in liquid guise,
Silent echoes, whispered sighs,
Crystals sparkle, lost in time,
Carving stories, soft as rhyme.

An underwater ballet sways,
As moonlight paints in silver rays,
Fishes glint like shards of stars,
In the silence, beauty soars.

Voices rise from the depths unknown,
Tales of wonders, lost but grown,
Each bubble carries distant dreams,
Fractured light on gentle streams.

In this realm of mystic depth,
Every heartbeat feels its breath,
A treasure trove of nature's grace,
Fragments of light in darkened space.

The Language of Sunbeams and Moss

When morning breaks, with golden hue,
Whispers travel, soft and true,
Sunbeams kiss the waking earth,
Igniting life, sparking rebirth.

Mossy blankets hold time's embrace,
Each tuft a story, each crease a trace,
Nature's tongue in tender tones,
A language spoken in hushed moans.

In hidden corners, secrets lie,
As flowers reach for the endless sky,
Rustling leaves share tales of old,
Rich with warmth, their peace unfolds.

Every shadow draped in light,
A painted canvas, morning bright,
The earth a book, each line a lore,
Sunshine dancing, forevermore.

Gather 'round, let hearts unite,
In the gentle glow of soft twilight,
With sunbeams weaving through the moss,
We find a world, not once, but across.

Glowing Threads of Magic in the Moss

In twilight's hush, the forest breathes,
Where soft green moss holds secrets deep.
Glowing threads twine 'round the leaves,
Whispering dreams that never sleep.

A flicker here, a shimmer there,
Mysteries dance upon the air.
As fairies spin with gentle grace,
Each spark ignites this enchanted place.

With every step, the shadows blend,
Into a tapestry unknown.
The magic weaves, it will not end,
In every heart, the truth is sown.

Under starlight, night unfolds,
The ancient stories come alive.
In glowing threads, the magic holds,
Where wonder wakes and spirits thrive.

So if you wander, heed the call,
Of mossy paths where dreamers glide.
For in each whisper, spells enthrall,
And through the woods, your heart will ride.

Whispers of the Verdant Glade

Deep within the verdant glade,
Leaves murmur softly, secrets shared.
With every breeze, the tales cascade,
As nature's voice sings unprepared.

Sunlight dances on emerald blades,
A symphony of light and shade.
Petals flutter, like soft parades,
In this realm where dreams are made.

Moss carpets earth in velvet hues,
While shadows play on ancient stone.
Each whispered word, a gentle muse,
Invites the weary heart back home.

Flowing streams weave through the trees,
Their laughter echoes, crystal clear.
A melody of sweet decrees,
Calling forth all who wander near.

So linger long, let time suspend,
In this glade where secrets lie.
With every breath, you'll comprehend,
Nature's magic under sky.

Secrets Woven in Sunbeams

In beams of light that break the morn,
Secrets hang like dew on leaves.
The world awakens, gently born,
In quietude, where magic weaves.

Golden threads of warmth cascade,
Through emerald boughs and flowered crowns.
In every ray, the sun is laid,
A tapestry where hope abounds.

Listen close to what they say,
In whispers soft, the heart can find.
A path unfolds where shadows play,
Glimpses of joy, so intertwined.

Every moment glows anew,
Where sunlight touches soil so sweet.
Secrets bloom in every hue,
In this dance of chaos, neat.

So seek the light, let worries cease,
Embrace the warmth that sets you free.
For in each sunbeam, find your peace,
A hidden world, where you can be.

Shadows Beneath the Ancient Canopy

In shadows cast by ancient trees,
Whispers linger in the dusk.
The forest hums with histories,
A treasure trove of dreams and musk.

Beneath the canopy so wide,
The world above fades into night.
The spirits of the woods abide,
In twinkling stars, they brush the light.

With every rustle, tales resound,
Of wanderers who sought their fate.
In every echo, wisdom found,
Where shadows hold the keys, innate.

Twisted roots and tangled vines,
Mark paths where few have dared to tread.
In twilight's glow, the magic shines,
In silent oaths the ancients said.

So when you roam this twilight place,
Remember well the tales unfold.
For deep within time's vast embrace,
The shadows keep their secrets bold.

Emerald Canopy Veils the Unseen

Beneath the emerald leaves so bright,
Mysteries linger hidden from sight.
Soft whispers weave through ancient trees,
A tapestry of rustling leaves.

Shadows dance on the forest floor,
Each step reveals a secret door.
With every breath, the wild sighs low,
In this realm where few dare to go.

Freaks of nature, adorned and rare,
Guardians of secrets, bond in pair.
In twilight's grasp, the magic thrives,
In every heartbeat, adventure survives.

Crickets sing their night-time tune,
Under the watchful eye of the moon.
The woodland spirits weave their art,
In emerald depths, they play their part.

Time meanders in twilight's breeze,
Whispers scatter like dancing leaves.
Each moment holds a tale untold,
In this emerald world, brave and bold.

Enchantment Lingers in the Stillness of Leaves

In stillness, enchantment softly flows,
A rhythm hidden where the forest grows.
Verdant canopies, a hushed refrain,
Embracing secrets wrapped in the grain.

Gentle breezes carry the sighs,
Of woodland spirits, their watchful eyes.
Foliage sways in the evening's grace,
An echo of laughter in nature's embrace.

Moonlight drapes a silvery hue,
Among the branches, where dreams come true.
The heart of the woods beats slow and deep,
In enchanted realms where magic keeps.

Each leaf a canvas, stories unfold,
Of timeless wonders, both brave and bold.
Through whispered winds, their voices blend,
A symphony of life that will never end.

Foliage Illuminates the Secrets of the Wild

Foliage dances with the sun's warm kiss,
Illuminating shadows, a fleeting bliss.
In tangled thickets where secrets dwell,
The whispers of nature weave their spell.

Glistening dew on petals bright,
Reflects the dawn's first gentle light.
A path through greenery, soft and wide,
Invites the wanderer to safely bide.

Creatures stir in the underbrush;
In harmony with nature, there's no rush.
Every rustle, every call,
Tells a tale of the wild, heard by all.

Sunset's palette, a blaze of delight,
Casts a glow on the approaching night.
In twilight's hush, the world transforms,
Wrapped in nature's enchanting charms.

Nature's Palette in a Whispering Glade

In a whispering glade, colors collide,
Nature's palette, a vibrant guide.
Hues of moss, emerald so pure,
Each shade a promise, sacred and sure.

Wildflowers sway in a lively dance,
Brought to life by chance and romance.
Petals flutter like wings in flight,
A canvas of beauty, a sheer delight.

The brook gurgles its joyous tune,
Reflecting the light of the silvery moon.
In this sanctuary, time stands still,
Awakening dreams with a gentle thrill.

The joy of the wild, forever alive,
In laughter of leaves, the heart shall thrive.
Under nature's brush, the world anew,
In a whispering glade, magic breaks through.

Radiant Beams Through Gnarled Branches

In the forest deep where whispers cling,
Radiant beams through the branches swing.
Golden sunlight skips on leaf and stone,
Nature's treasure, a world of its own.

Mossy carpets beneath ancient trees,
Laughter echoes in soft summer breeze.
Gnarled fingers stretch to the sky above,
In the heart of the wild, there's magic and love.

Shadows dance in a waltz of delight,
Painting the ground with a soft, warm light.
Each petal glistens like treasures untold,
In the embrace where wonders unfold.

A chattering brook hums a sweet song,
To the rhythm of nature, it all belongs.
Every branch tells tales of ages past,
In the twilight glow, these moments last.

So wander beneath this enchanted sky,
Where the gnarled branches and dreams fly high.
With each step taken upon this bright scene,
You'll find the magic that lies in between.

Spells Cast by Flickering Light

In the heart of the night, the candles flicker,
Whispers of magic grow ever thicker.
Spells cast gently on the night air,
With a shimmer of stars that beckons us there.

Each soft flicker, a story unfurls,
A dance of shadows, a swirl of whirls.
Words drape like silk, their power ignites,
As dreams intertwine in the hush of the nights.

Moonbeams weave through the windows so wide,
Guiding lost souls to the magic inside.
With potions and trinkets arranged all around,
In this flickering glow, enchantment is found.

Starlit secrets seep into our hearts,
As each laugh and each sigh, the magic imparts.
The air turns electric with every soft spark,
In the realm of the night, there's no room for dark.

So gather your wishes and let them take flight,
With spells cast by love in the flickering light.
The world awaits just beyond the door,
Step into the magic, discover much more.

Dreamcatchers of Sunlit Patches

Beneath the wandering clouds so high,
Dreamcatchers dance where sunbeams lie.
They gather the dreams of those lost in thought,
Amidst the warm patches of bliss they sought.

With threads of gold and whispers of grace,
They weave an embrace, a soft, sacred space.
In the laughter of children and rustle of leaves,
The heart finds its solace, the soul gently weaves.

Every twinkle of light, a wish on the way,
To catch all the shadows that threaten to stay.
Sunlit patches, a canvas so bright,
Creating a tapestry stitched with delight.

The colors blend softly, like dawn's gentle glow,
Bringing forth stories only dreamers know.
With each whispered secret, each sigh that's released,
The world spins anew, and the heart finds its peace.

So sway with the breeze in this enchanted glade,
Where dreamcatchers flourish and hope won't fade.
Bathe in the warmth of the sun's golden rays,
For this is the land where the magic stays.

Twilight's Embrace Among the Trees

In the tender twilight, shadows arise,
Embraced by the trees under softening skies.
The world sighs a hush as the day gives way,
To secrets and dreams in soft shades of gray.

Branches intertwine, a gentle embrace,
Guardians of whispers, the heart's sacred space.
Stars peek with wonder at the earth below,
In twilight's glow, magic starts to flow.

With each rustle of leaves, the air comes alive,
As the fireflies flicker and softly dive.
Nature's orchestra plays a soothing tune,
With each note of twilight, the heart begins to swoon.

A kiss of the wind on a lover's soft cheek,
In the stillness of dusk, the soul learns to speak.
Every heartbeat dances in sync with the night,
In this sanctuary, everything feels right.

So wander beneath stars in the deepening shade,
Let twilight's embrace be the path that you've made.
In the arms of the trees, find your heart's quiet plea,
For in this enchanted world, you are forever free.

The Glow of Nature's Heart

In the gentle hush of dawn's embrace,
Whispers of magic fill the space.
With every leaf that shimmers bright,
Nature's heart beats pure delight.

In the dewdrops hung on blades of grass,
Mirrors of worlds that come to pass.
Crickets sing their soft, sweet song,
In this realm where dreams belong.

Under the boughs, where shadows play,
Life dances in a sprightly sway.
Petals twirl in the morning glow,
Every petal, a story to know.

The brook babbles with joyful glee,
A tune as old as you and me.
Each ripple holds a tale of yore,
Nature's heart forevermore.

Sunlit Paths Through Mystic Woods

Sunlit paths weave through ancient trees,
Where whispered secrets ride the breeze.
Each step unveils a hidden cheer,
As fables spring to life right here.

Golden beams through leaves cascade,
Casting shadows, a playful charade.
The forest breathes, a living dream,
With every sound, my heart will beam.

Mossy carpets beneath my feet,
Each crunch of twigs, a symphony sweet.
Birdsong lilts in the cool, crisp air,
A magic found most anywhere.

Twisting trails lead to surprise,
Enchanting wonders before my eyes.
In dappled light, the world feels new,
Whispers of dreams in every view.

An Ode to the Glimmering Underbrush

In shadows deep where secrets lie,
The underbrush begins to sigh.
With every rustle, every breeze,
Mysteries dance among the trees.

Tiny creatures dart and play,
Glistening gems of the forest's sway.
Amidst the leaves, a world unfolds,
In its embrace, adventure holds.

Ferns unfurl with grace and might,
Adorning earth in emerald light.
Each tendril tells a story grand,
Of life and depth in nature's hand.

Beneath the canopy's warm embrace,
Glimmers of life find their place.
In this realm where shadows flow,
Every glance reveals new glow.

Nature's Glints in a Hidden Nest

High in the branches, a nest is cradled,
Where dreams of spring are gently tangled.
Feathers soft and twigs interlace,
In this sanctuary, a warm embrace.

Whispers of life amidst the leaves,
A cocooned magic that never deceives.
Tiny hearts beat a rapid tune,
As dawn brings light from silver moon.

The world outside hums a lively beat,
Yet here is where the stillness greets.
Each flutter speaks of love's sweet song,
In this haven where we belong.

Nature's glints in every nest,
A promise of life, a whispered quest.
Beneath the canopy, life unfolds,
In whispered tales, its magic holds.

The Harmony of Luminous Growth

In gardens where the soft winds play,
The flowers dance in bright array.
Each petal kissed by morning's dew,
A symphony of colors, pure and true.

Among the roots, the secrets lie,
Of whispered dreams that never die.
In every leaf, a story's spun,
Revealing beauty to anyone.

The sun above, a guiding light,
Mends broken hearts, ignites the night.
In unity, the earth does sing,
Of harmony in everything.

When twilight drapes the world in grace,
The stars emerge to take their place.
With each soft glow, the shadows fade,
As nature's music serenades.

So linger long, let spirits soar,
In places where the wildflowers pour.
And find in blooms, both near and far,
The harmony of who we are.

Gentle Touch of Celestial Spheres

In twilight's kiss, the heavens shine,
With stars that whisper tales divine.
Each twinkle holds a secret grace,
A gentle touch from time and space.

The moonlight bathes the earth in dreams,
Where silver threads weave silent themes.
In starlit paths, the souls may roam,
Finding light, and calling it home.

Beneath the arch of velvet night,
The cosmos hums, a pure delight.
With planetary waltz, they sway,
Entwined in dark, yet bright as day.

Each comet brings a wish anew,
With fleeting trails in skies so blue.
In cosmic dance, we join the play,
With hearts aglow, we find our way.

So gaze above as dreams unfold,
In the celestial, brave and bold.
Let starlit wonders fill your view,
With gentle touch, we'll carry through.

Mystical Light at the Forest's Edge

Where shadows twine with morning mist,
Lies a path that none could resist.
Each step reveals a tale untold,
In whispered secrets, ancient, old.

The sunlight weaves a golden thread,
Through leafy canopies up ahead.
Enchanting hues of emerald glow,
A tapestry where dreams may flow.

Along the banks, a stream does sing,
With songs of joy the forest brings.
In sparkling drops, the bright dew gleams,
Reflecting all of nature's dreams.

With creatures stirring, wild and free,
The heartbeat dances, pure esprit.
In every rustling leaf and sigh,
The forest breathes; it can deny.

So venture forth to where it leads,
For magic's found in simple deeds.
At edge of woods, where light does blend,
Mystical paths and wonders mend.

The Mirage of Glade and Glow

In a glade where shadows linger near,
A spark of magic soon appears.
With flickering lights that softly sway,
The dreams of night begin to play.

Beneath the boughs, the whispers rise,
As fireflies dance under twilight skies.
In shimmering clusters, they weave a tale,
Of wanderers lost, on a mystic trail.

Each flicker hints at secrets kept,
In the heart of woods where spirits slept.
The echoes of laughter fill the night,
In this mirage of glade and light.

So follow the glow through the leafy doors,
Where enchantments flow, and joy restores.
In twilight's heart, let wonders reign,
For dreams alight, like softest rain.

With gentle steps, and hearts aglow,
You'll find the paths of ebb and flow.
In mirages bright, the truth will flow,
A place where magic always grows.

Enchanted Light Filtering Through Leaves

In the grove where secrets play,
Sunbeams dance in bright array,
Whispers rustle through the trees,
A gentle sigh upon the breeze.

Flickering shades in emerald hue,
Nature's canvas, rich and true,
Branches arch like graceful hands,
Holding magic in their strands.

Golden drops of light cascade,
Painting paths where shadows fade,
A symphony of light and shade,
In this realm where dreams are made.

Each petal glows with stories old,
Tales of wonder to be told,
As the day begins to wane,
With every leaf, a soft refrain.

Here in this enchanted glade,
Time stands still, and fears allayed,
Nature's heart, so wild and free,
Holds a charm that beckons me.

Glimmers of Magic Among the Roots

Deep within the tangled earth,
Lies a place of ancient birth,
Glimmers twinkle, faint yet bright,
Echoes of a hidden light.

Roots entwined in silent grace,
Guard the magic in their place,
Every sprout, a mystic sign,
Vibrations of the divine.

Mushrooms rise with caps aglow,
In the twilight, secrets flow,
Luminous whispers, soft and clear,
Call to those who dare draw near.

Colored lights dance through the air,
In this realm of dreams laid bare,
To the rhythm of the night,
Boundless wonders take their flight.

In the shadows, stories bloom,
Haunting notes in twilight's room,
Where the roots weave tales anew,
Magic thrives in every hue.

Luminous Echoes in the Woodland

In the woodland's twilight glow,
Luminous echoes start to flow,
Every footfall whispers low,
As enchanted spirits show.

Branches weave a golden thread,
Where the fearless dare to tread,
Hushed enchantments softly sound,
In this hallowed, sacred ground.

Crickets chant a nightly song,
To the rhythm, we belong,
Underneath the starry dome,
Find a world that feels like home.

Glistening dew on leaves adorned,
In the magic, hearts reborn,
Shimmering promises abound,
In these echoes, joy is found.

Nature's breath, a tender sigh,
As the night wraps 'round the sky,
In this space, our souls align,
With the secret paths we find.

Beneath the Emerald Veil of Dreams

Beneath the emerald veil we tread,
Whispers linger, softly said,
In this world of gentle aisles,
Dreams entwined in nature's smiles.

Dappled shadows weave their cloak,
Veiling magic in each stroke,
A tapestry of emerald green,
Where the heart finds joy unseen.

Every flower holds a thought,
Of the battles bravely fought,
As we wander, hand in hand,
Where the earth and dreams expand.

Misty tendrils, softly glow,
Guide us where the fairies flow,
In this realm, we dance and sway,
Lost within the bright bouquet.

In the evening's tender sigh,
Magic lingers, floating high,
Beneath the veil, our spirits gleam,
Together, living every dream.

Sylvan Secrets Unfurled

In the heart of the forest, whispers sing,
Beneath emerald canopies, secrets take wing.
Ancient trees with stories abound,
While the curious creatures dance all around.

Moonlight weaves through shadows so deep,
Lulling the wild to a slumbering sleep.
The rustle of leaves, a soothing refrain,
Revealing the magic that courses like rain.

Each glade and glimmer, a tale to impart,
Enchanting the dreamers, a spell on the heart.
From roots entwined to twinkling stars,
The sylvan songs whisper of wonders from afar.

Soft footfalls of faeries, they shimmer and glide,
In the tapestry woven where secrets abide.
With every soft sigh of the silvery breeze,
The secrets of sylva bring boundless ease.

Radiance Among the Ferns

Beneath the fronds where ferns unfold,
Lies a tapestry woven in emerald and gold.
Glimmers of sunlight, a playful tease,
Dancing on petals with effortless ease.

Each droplet of dew, a sparkling gem,
Holds the world's secrets, a delicate hymn.
The air is alive with the fragrance of earth,
Celebrating nature's mysterious birth.

A breeze carries whispers; leaves softly sway,
Filling the forest with laughter and play.
In shadows where magic and wonder unite,
Radiance twinkles, igniting the night.

Hidden in corners, the magic is found,
As creatures emerge from their sheltering ground.
In harmony, life threads its radiant song,
Among the ferns, where the heart feels it strong.

The Dappled Dance of Sunlight

In the morning light, a shimmer ignites,
Through branches it weaves, a tapestry bright.
Dappled patterns on leaves, they do sway,
Whispering tales of the dawning day.

Golden beams play with shadows so bold,
Caressing the earth with warmth to unfold.
The dance of the sunlight, a magical show,
Guiding the wanderers, on paths they do go.

As hourglass sands slip away from their grip,
Fleeting moments in nature's soft script.
A symphony crafted by sun's gentle hand,
All creatures rejoice in this luminous land.

Amidst the grand oaks, the light's gentle kiss,
Harvests of laughter, pure moments of bliss.
The dappled dance celebrates life in its form,
Creating a world both alive and warm.

Beneath the Twilight Canopy

As the sun bows low, the twilight descends,
Soft shadows weave where the day softly ends.
The canopy thickens, a blanket of night,
Where magic awakens, and dreams take flight.

Stars peek through boughs, twinkling with glee,
Illuminating secrets held deep in the tree.
A breeze carries stories, soft-spoken lore,
Of lands far away and adventures galore.

The night creatures stir in their silent ballet,
Cloaked in the moonlight, they leap, sway, and play.
Echoes of hoots and the rustle of wings,
Remind us of wonder, the joy the night brings.

Beneath this vast dome, the heart feels at home,
In the depths of the woodland, no need to roam.
For each passing moment, a gift to behold,
In the twilight's embrace, life's wonders unfold.

Interlaced Shadows and Sun

In the glen where whispers play,
Shadows dance with golden light.
Branches weave a soft ballet,
Day and night entwine their flight.

Dreams unfurl on gentle breeze,
Secrets linger on the lane.
Rustling leaves among the trees,
Each note sings a sweet refrain.

Footsteps trace the timeless path,
Mossy stones that tell a tale.
Nature's pulse, a quiet wrath,
In the hush, the heart's set sail.

With each breath, the world unfurls,
Magic twirls in every sigh.
Golden dust like spun-out pearls,
In this realm where spirits fly.

Holding tight to fleeting hours,
Memories like gilded suns.
Beneath this frame of leafy bowers,
Life's sweet symphony still runs.

Lush Serenity Underneath the Canopy

Beneath the boughs, where shadows sigh,
A tapestry of emerald hue.
Nature hums a lullaby,
Telling tales both old and new.

Sunbeams pierce the leafy veil,
Dancing on the forest floor.
Gentle whispers weave a trail,
Guiding souls to tranquil shore.

Woodland creatures softly roam,
In their eyes, the wisdom glows.
This serene and sacred home,
Where the river of life flows.

Fungi flourish, wildflowers sprout,
A kingdom rich with colors bright.
In this haven, doubt's cast out,
And the world feels pure and right.

Holding whispers of the past,
Every step, a story shared.
In this comfort, shadows cast,
Peace and joy, forever paired.

Veiled Radiance of the Woodland Heart

In the stillness, silence speaks,
A gentle pulse beneath the ground.
Veiled in mystery, nature seeks,
Wonders lost, now found, profound.

Veins of light through trees do thread,
Each glimmer holds a secret bright.
Where dreams and daylight softly wed,
Boundless realms in whispers light.

Harmonies of rustling leaves,
Softly echo in the night.
Underneath the moon's reprieve,
Stars imbue the world with light.

Every shadow tells a tale,
Of ancient paths worn by the wise.
Where the heartbeats softly pale,
Beneath vast and watchful skies.

Through the woodlands, spirits glide,
Carried forth on breezes warm.
In this glade, our joys abide,
Nature's peace, a steadfast charm.

Empress of the Emerald Shadows

In twilight's depth, she takes her throne,
Emerald shadows cloak her grace.
Among the branches, winds have blown,
A silent majesty in place.

Eyes like stars, alight with dreams,
Beneath the boughs, she softly glides.
Her laughter flows in bubbling streams,
Enchanting all who roam her guides.

With every step, the earth does sigh,
Rich and vibrant, life unfolds.
In the embrace of time gone by,
Whispers of magic still retold.

Wrapped in fables, aged like wine,
Every leaf holds tales so rare.
The woodland's heart, a sacred shrine,
Where beauty flows beyond compare.

Empress of all hidden things,
Guardian of the dusk and dawn.
In her realm, the wildheart sings,
And in shadows, dreams are drawn.

Lush Dreams in the Twilight Thicket

In twilight's grasp, where shadows blend,
Whispers of dreams in the soft night send.
Foxgloves dance with a gentle grace,
As stars awaken in a secret place.

Moonlit paths wound through the trees,
Kissed by a breeze, a tender tease.
Each leaf a tale of the night unseen,
Where magic lingers in shades of green.

Silvery streams that giggle and twirl,
Crickets play where the fireflies swirl.
A tapestry woven with whispers and sighs,
In this enchanted land where the heart flies.

Mysteries beckon from thickets deep,
Guarded by creatures that softly creep.
Their silent watch in this leafy dome,
Under the stars, where dreams find home.

Sleep comes easy in twilight's embrace,
Cradled in wonder, in this secret place.
Where stories bloom like flowers in spring,
In lush dreams hidden, the nightbirds sing.

Where Time Pauses in Shaded Delights

In a glade where the sunbeams play,
Time suspends, in a magical way.
Petals drift on a whispering breeze,
Secrets shared beneath ancient trees.

Mossy carpets invite wandering feet,
Softly cushioning where the shadows meet.
Gentle laughter of streams nearby,
Echoes the joy of the birds in the sky.

Each rustling leaf holds a tale of old,
Of lovers who dreamed, of heroes bold.
In the quiet pulse of the emerald light,
The forest hums with splendid delight.

Dappled sun like a painter's brush,
Fills the world with a silken hush.
Where time forgets its hurried race,
And moments linger in nature's grace.

Here lies a treasure both pure and bright,
In the heart of the wood, where all is right.
Where magic breathes in softest sights,
And time pauses in shaded delights.

The Shimmer of Life in Forgotten Places

In corners dim where shadows weave,
Life's shimmer sparkles, hard to believe.
Crumbling walls with stories untold,
Whisper of dreams in the twilight gold.

Vines clutch tightly, the stones they embrace,
Nature reclaiming its verdant space.
A fluttering wing, a whispering breeze,
Brings forth the magic that comforts and frees.

Through cracked old windows, the light streams in,
A tapestry spun thick with loss and kin.
Echoes of laughter, of love and of strife,
In these forgotten places, there's light in life.

Muffled footsteps of long-gone souls,
In haunting beauty, the past extolls.
Each cranny and crevice holds visions bright,
Where shadows dance in the soft golden light.

Hearts are tethered to moments once shared,
In dim-lit corners where time never cared.
In the shimmer of life, memories trace,
A lingering warmth in forgotten place.

Light Weaves Through the Tangle of Green

Through tendrils thick, where wild things grow,
Soft light weaves in with a radiant glow.
Each beam a ribbon of golden thread,
Penetrating depths where the earth's heart bled.

Ferns unfurl in a caressing dance,
Inviting the sun for a fleeting glance.
The chorus of life, a sweet serenade,
In the tangle of green, where dreams are made.

A dive of a bird, a rustling hare,
Nature's symphony fills the warm air.
In the rustle and hush, the world comes alive,
As light weaves through, and the wild things thrive.

Glimmers of hope in each leaf and vine,
Whispers of magic in every line.
The intricate dance of nature unfolds,
With stories of old that the forest holds.

So take a moment, linger awhile,
In the embrace of the woods, find your smile.
For in the tangle where the wild things preen,
The heart finds its peace in the tangle of green.

Gleeful Twinkles Among the Twigs

In the hush of dawn's embrace,
Twinkling lights dance with grace,
Among the twigs, joy takes flight,
Whispers soft, a pure delight.

Silver dew with sparkles bright,
Cascades of dreams take gentle height,
Every rustle, a giggle shared,
Nature's secrets, lightly bared.

Children of the woodland fair,
Chasing echoes that fill the air,
With laughter sweet and spirits bold,
Stories of old begin to unfold.

A tapestry of emerald hue,
Where shadows play and winds pursue,
Each moment sings, a vibrant song,
In this hidden world where we belong.

Gleeful twinkles, hearts ignite,
Captured in the morning light,
The forest hums a lively tune,
Beneath the sway of the silvered moon.

Celestial Whispers Behind the Bark

In the depth of evening's sigh,
Stars awaken, gleaming high,
Behind the bark, old tales unfurl,
A cosmic dance, a secret swirl.

Murmurs soft as stardust flows,
Ancient echoes, timeless prose,
The moonlight bathes the sacred ground,
Where magic lives and dreams are found.

Shimmering dust on leaves does gleam,
The air is filled with endless dreams,
Celestial whispers, gentle grace,
Enveloping us in a warm embrace.

Through the branches, shadows weave,
In this shelter, hearts believe,
Time extends its tender hand,
In this enchanted, timeless land.

The universe sings soft and clear,
Melodies for those who dare near,
Behind the bark, the stories tell,
Of love, of loss, and the magic spell.

Murmurs of Light in the Forest

When twilight falls, a whisper glows,
In the hush where the wild wind blows,
Murmurs of light dance on the stream,
Casting shadows, weaving a dream.

A tapestry of amber hues,
Each glimmer shares a tale of truths,
The trees nod softly, wisdom deep,
Guardians of secrets they keep.

Fleeting moments, history's breath,
A celebration of life and death,
In the clearing where spirits twine,
The stars above begin to shine.

Step lightly, wanderer, take your time,
In this realm where rhythms rhyme,
Murmurs of light will guide your way,
Through night's embrace into the day.

The forest speaks in hues and tones,
Offering warmth like ancient bones,
In each rustle, a promise bright,
Awaits the heart that seeks the light.

A Play of Shadows on Ancient Stones

On ancient stones where dreams have tread,
Whispers weave of words unsaid,
A play of shadows, twilight glows,
Where memories linger, time bestows.

Silhouettes dance, a soft ballet,
Echoes of laughter from yesterday,
Cloaked in dusk, the stones reveal,
Their silent stories, a world surreal.

With each footstep, history stirs,
In this hallowed ground, wonder blurs,
The air is thick with twilight's kiss,
A gentle pull, a certain bliss.

Every shadow speaks in sighs,
Melodies of the moonlit skies,
The stones, a witness to the night,
Invite the heart to dance in light.

In the sacred space where echoes dwell,
Weaves a magic no words can tell,
Λ symphony of whispers grown,
A timeless tale in the shadows shown.

Ethereal Glows in Hidden Groves

In twilight's grasp, the whispers weave,
Where ancient trees and shadows grieve.
Soft luminescence paints the dark,
As fireflies dance, a fleeting spark.

Beneath the canopies, secrets sigh,
Each breath of wind, a gentle cry.
The moon peeks through with silvery grace,
Illuminating this enchanted place.

The ground is rich with tales untold,
Of fae and dreams and legends old.
In quiet moments, magic stirs,
A symphony of rustling furs.

Each glimmer shows a path less known,
Through thickets thick, where wonders grown.
With every step, a spell we cast,
In twilight's arms, our shadows last.

So linger here, where time stands still,
In hidden groves, our hearts fulfill.
Ethereal glows, in night's embrace,
We find ourselves in nature's grace.

Mystic Beams on Velvet Moss

Upon the forest floor, mossy beds,
Where ancient footfalls mark the spreads.
Bright beams break through the leafy shrouds,
Bathing the earth in emerald crowds.

With every step, the soft quest calls,
As morning light through canopy falls.
A tapestry of colors bright,
We wander on, enchanted by light.

The whispered stories of the trees,
Float gently on the playful breeze.
In every bloom, a dream to seek,
In nature's heart, where spirits speak.

With every breath, a treasure found,
In the serene, where peace abounds.
Mystic beams guide our way,
Through velvet moss, we choose to stay.

The magic here, an endless sigh,
In twilight glows beneath the sky.
The world transforms in nature's thrall,
In simple beauty, we find it all.

Chasing Light Through Woodland Shadows

In dappled light, where shadows dance,
We chase the day, a fleeting chance.
The forest calls with secret lore,
In every glimpse, we seek for more.

A winding path under towering trees,
Where sunlight kisses, and cool winds tease.
Through thickets thick and hidden lanes,
Adventure whispers, unbroken chains.

With every turn, new sights appear,
The pulse of nature, pure and clear.
In realms of green, with hearts so light,
We wander far, embracing night.

The shadows blend with evening's grace,
In twilight's glow, we find our place.
Chasing light, we slip away,
Into the dreams of end of day.

With laughter shared and spirits bold,
In woodland realms, our hearts unfold.
Each hidden glen, a story spun,
In chasing light, our souls are won.

The Spell of Glistening Green

Oh, spellbound earth of vibrant hue,
With glistening green and skies so blue.
In every leaf, the magic flows,
A world alive where wildness grows.

As sunlight drips from branches high,
A rare enchantment fills the sky.
Each droplet caught in morning's glow,
Holds whispered secrets, soft and slow.

In grassy meadows, spirits twine,
A dance of beings, sweet and divine.
Weaving through the fragrant air,
In glistening green, we shed our care.

The heartbeat of the woods we seek,
In every sigh, the earth will speak.
Embraced by wonder, we are free,
In nature's spell, our hearts agree.

The world transforms in shades of grace,
In every step, the wild embrace.
Glistening green, where dreams convene,
The magic here, forever seen.

Gleaming Secrets of the Green Night

In twilight's hush, the shadows weave,
Whispers of dreams that night conceives.
Moonbeams dance on emerald glade,
Stirring secrets, softly laid.

A gentle breeze through branches sighs,
As starlit wonders fill the skies.
Mysteries wrapped in silver threads,
Await the paths where magic treads.

The forest hums with tales untold,
Of ancient woods, both warm and cold.
Each rustle holds a silent plea,
For hearts that hold the night's decree.

Painted skies of azure hue,
Guard hidden truths in twilight's dew.
The night unfolds its velvet cloak,
In the embrace where shadows soak.

Beneath the arch of twilight's throne,
Gleaming secrets call us home.
In the quiet, find the light,
That guides us through the green night.

The Sun's Soft Sigh in the Glade

The morning breaks with whispers sweet,
As golden rays begin to greet.
In harmony with nature's song,
The sun's soft sigh, where hearts belong.

Among the trees, with leaves adorned,
A canvas of dreams, gently born.
Petals unfurl in morning's glow,
As time takes pause, and worries go.

Reflections dance in trickling streams,
Where every ripple holds our dreams.
The glade, a haven, pure and bright,
Bathed in warmth of morning light.

A symphony of life unfolds,
In gentle hues of greens and golds.
Every whisper invites us near,
To listen close, to feel, to hear.

So linger long in nature's grace,
In the sun's soft sigh, embrace.
Every heartbeat sings anew,
In the glade where dreams come true.

Reflections of a Sylvan Dream

In the depths of the whispering wood,
Where every sigh is understood.
Reflections bloom in twilight's kiss,
Silent echoes of timeless bliss.

Old oaks stand with stories wide,
Guardians of the glen's soft side.
Each shadow weaves a tapestry,
Of secrets held eternally.

A symphony of leaves does play,
As sunlight dances, fades away.
In this realm where dreams ignite,
Shadows blend in pure delight.

Beneath the stars, the cosmos gleams,
A canvas painted with our dreams.
In the heart of nature's grace,
Reflections found in this sacred space.

Join the song beneath the moon,
In sylvan dreams, our hearts attune.
The night's embrace whispers clear,
Inviting us to linger near.

Enigmas of Light Among the Leaves

Beneath the boughs, where secrets lie,
Enigmas stir beneath the sky.
With every flutter, whispers flow,
In laughter dancing, soft and low.

The light cascades in golden beams,
Awakening the forest's dreams.
In shadows deep, where echoes blend,
Mysteries linger, never end.

A world where fairies steal the night,
And fireflies weave their tales of light.
In the heart of leaves, we seek the truth,
Of timeless magic, ageless youth.

Each rustling leaf, each secret murmur,
Holds stories spun in memory's fervor.
In the dance of dusk, let us find,
The enchantments woven, intertwined.

So wander here, where light unfolds,
And every shadow, a story holds.
Among the leaves, delightful tease,
We chase the enigmas of the breeze.

Whims of Nature in the Quiet Grove

In the quiet grove where willows sway,
Whispers of breeze weave tales each day.
Sunlight dapples through leaves so green,
In shadows deep, secrets are seen.

A brook babbles soft, a songbird trills,
Nature's orchestra dances and spills.
Gentle ferns unfurl with grace,
In this hidden, enchanted place.

Mushrooms sprout in hues so bright,
Glowing softly under silver light.
Dewdrops gleam like diamonds rare,
In the stillness, magic fills the air.

Beneath the arch of ancient trees,
Fluttering leaves take to the breeze.
Creatures stir in the evening glow,
In the grove, life ebbs and flows.

With every step, adventures gleam,
In a world woven from a dream.
The quiet grove, a sanctuary found,
Where nature's wonders abound.

Luminescence of the Understory's Heart

In the darkened woods where shadows play,
Glowing embers chase the night away.
Fungi bloom in colors bright,
A dance of jewels, a magical sight.

Luminous trails lead onward, bold,
Whispers of stories yet untold.
Creeping vines in velvet embrace,
Nestle creatures in their warm space.

Fireflies twinkle, stars in flight,
Painting the dusk with flickering light.
Among the roots, the secrets lie,
In the heart of the earth, dreams sigh.

Each rustling leaf, a soft-spoken vow,
To the wonders that see us now.
Nature's thrum, a pulsing beat,
In the stillness, magic does meet.

As dawn approaches with glimmers of gold,
The tales of the night will gently unfold.
Understory whispers, lives entwined,
In the depths of the wood, beauty defined.

Dreamlike Suspensions Among the Roots

Suspended dreams hang thick in the air,
Among the roots, memories ensnare.
Twisting tendrils cradling the past,
Each moment in time, an echo vast.

Nestled deep in the earth's embrace,
Secrets linger in every space.
Moss carpets the forest floor,
Soft as whispers that time implores.

A thrum of life beneath our feet,
Echoes of seasons, a rhythmic beat.
Through tangled paths, adventures weave,
In twilight's glow, we dare believe.

Glimmers of echoes, ancient and wise,
Guide our hearts to the moonlit skies.
Suspended moments, breath held tight,
In the hush of woods, all feels right.

With every step, a tale unfolds,
In the arms of roots, wisdom holds.
Dreamlike journeys beckon us near,
Whispers of nature, for all to hear.

Pictures of Wonder in Leafy Abodes

In leafy abodes where the magic gleams,
Pictures of wonder spark our dreams.
Among the branches, in cradled nests,
Life flourishes in nature's best.

Squirrel and rabbit dart here and there,
Among the ferns, they dance with flair.
Colors of petals, so vivid, so bright,
Adorn the woods in morning light.

Each sunlight beam, a painter divine,
Strokes of warmth, on everyone shine.
In riverbanks lush, reflections play,
The canvas of nature, alive each day.

Gathering songs on a soft summer's eve,
Nature's chorus, a heart to believe.
Every breeze carries whispers so sweet,
With every moment, life's rhythm repeats.

In the forest's heart, where wonder resides,
Pictures of magic, our hearts it guides.
Amidst leafy abodes, our spirits find peace,
In nature's embrace, our worries release.

Flickers of Hope in Green Embraces

In the heart of the whispering woods,
Dreams twinkle, like stars in a night.
Beneath the boughs, hope subtly broods,
Casting shadows, a shimmering light.

Gentle breezes carry secrets sweet,
Where sunlight dances, embracing the ground.
Each petal and leaf, a tale to repeat,
In whispers of love, the lost may be found.

A stream flows softly, a silken song,
Reflecting the wishes of hearts ever true.
Binding the fragile, yet vibrant, along,
In emerald pathways, old and anew.

In twilight's glow, where the ferns assimilate,
With each soft rustle, there's magic to see.
The forest's pulse, an enchanting fate,
Invites weary souls to simply be free.

When shadows loom and the night hangs low,
Beneath ancient canopies, fears softly sway.
The flickers of hope, in warm green glow,
Guide the lost wanderers, lighting their way.

Wilderness Speaks in Subtle Glows

Amidst the tangled vines and leaves,
Whispers echo through the air.
The wild speaks softly, yet deeply believes,
In secrets hidden, waiting to share.

Moonlight seeps through branches, so old,
Illuminating paths with a silver sheen.
Each shadow dancing, a story untold,
In the night's embrace, where the forest is keen.

Crickets serenade the coming dusk,
Their melodies weave through the trees so tall.
In the wilderness, life sheds its husk,
As the universe listens, responding to all.

Stars peek through with a twinkling smile,
The brush of twilight, a soft caress.
In this wild realm, time lingers a while,
As nature unfolds her secrets, we guess.

With every rustle and faint breath of breeze,
The wilderness beckons, strong and serene.
In shadows and glows, we find inner peace,
Trusting the whispers that lie in between.

Fern-laden Echoes of Light

Under the canopy, where shadows merge,
Ferns unfold their elegance wide.
A dance of green, like life's gentle surge,
In this tranquil haven, we abide.

Sunbeams filter like whispers of fate,
Kissing the earth, igniting the scene.
The echoes of laughter, the heart's soft state,
In this fern-laden realm, pure and evergreen.

Moss carpets the ground, lush and alive,
Each step a reminder of beauty's grace.
In nature's embrace, we dare to thrive,
Finding our rhythm in this sacred space.

With every breath, a story unspools,
Written in leaves, a tale bold and bright.
The forest holds wisdom, guiding our rules,
In the fern-laden echoes, we'll find our light.

So linger awhile where the forest is deep,
Let time unwind amidst emerald blades.
For in every sigh, in each secret we keep,
The language of nature serenely cascades.

Greenery's Guardian: The Radiant Shade

In the realm of green, where shadows play,
Guardians rise beneath the sun's golden fold.
Each leaf a protector in its own way,
Providing solace, tender and bold.

Under the arch of ancient trees,
Whispers of wisdom drift upon the air.
The softness of green brings gentle ease,
While sunlight weaves through, weaving a prayer.

In hidden glades, where the coolness reigns,
A sanctuary woven with love and care.
Nature's sweet heart, free from worldly chains,
Nurturing souls, binding earth with the air.

Through every season, from bloom to fall,
The guardians stand, steadfast and strong.
In their embrace, we feel the call,
To venture through life, wherever we belong.

So dance with the shadows, find joy in the shade,
For greenery shelters dreams with delight.
In the arms of the forest, we're never afraid,
In this radiant realm, everything feels right.

www.ingramcontent.com/pod-product-compliance
Ingram Content Group UK Ltd.
Pitfield, Milton Keynes, MK11 3LW, UK
UKHW021440290125
4349UKWH00039B/558

9 781805 639442